bloom.

*a collection of poems that will
take you on a heartfelt journey
of love, loss, and hope.*

myah davidson

Bloom.

poems by
Myah Davidson

ISBN 978-1-09831-429-3

Cover photograph by Maxine Ficheux
Interior design by tamiboyce.com

she blooms.
even when darkness engulfs her.

—becca lee

bloom.

contents

love

bloom.

you are mine.

today,

tomorrow,

and forever.

bloom.

though we go through our ups and downs,

and we both get annoyed with each other,

i wouldn't trade it for the world,

because what comes after, makes up for all of it.

bloom.

what is the best feeling in the world?

he asked.

the best feeling in the world would have to be when i'm with you.

bloom.

my heart.

my heart can take anything.

no matter the situation.

it beats.

but it gets tired.

it aches.

it breaks.

but, the best thing my heart can do is love you, unconditionally.

bloom.

you are my sunshine.

you are the one with me dancing in the rain.

you care for me like no one else ever does, so please don't leave
me in the dust.

myah davidson

bloom.

a home doesn't have to consist of walls and windows.

at least my home doesn't.

my home consists of two arms and a heartbeat.

bloom.

what is love?

do you want to know what love is?

love is the person you want to spend the rest of your life with.

love is sharing your deepest thoughts and feelings with them,

and knowing they won't make fun of you.

love is also, getting a text from them in the middle of the day just
to let you know they are thinking about you.

lastly, what love is, is loving that person endlessly, through the
good and bad times.

bloom.

treat yourself how you would love
someone.

bloom.

there is nothing wrong with putting yourself first.

bloom.

i don't want to lose you.

i don't want to let go of you.

i want to keep holding on to you,

forever, or as long as i can.

i know we aren't together, and we won't be,

but you will always be mine, until the end of time.

bloom.

that night i sent you a random picture of my bathroom drawer.

who would've thought it would start something.

out of all the things you could've noticed, you noticed that.

the yellow perfume bottle with the sunflower on top, and it was
  labeled "daisy love."

you said back, "i like the smell of that perfume with the
  sunflower on top."

and after you told me that, that's all i wore.

bloom.

i want to be your number one.

i want to be your go-to text to get ice cream.

i want to be your biggest fan.

i want to be the reason you can't sleep when we are in a fight.

i want to be the lips you always want to kiss.

i want to be the scent you crave.

i want to be the shoulder you cry on when you need one.

and i want to be that someone you go to when you need a laugh.

but most importantly, i want to be your everything.

bloom.

could i ever live without you?

the answer is no.

even if we part ways, you will always have a piece of my heart,

no matter what.

we shared our kisses, we shared our deepest feelings, and we

shared our love.

i will cherish those memories,

and i will love you til the end of time.

bloom.

when did you start getting into poetry?

why do you like it so much? it's just so deep, her mom said.

after he broke my heart.

mom, poetry can put my thoughts into words better than i can.

bloom.

i want to say; you will always have a place in my heart.

loss

bloom.

you were my first love.

my first butterfly feeling.

my first hand i held.

my first real hug.

my first movie double date.

my first lips i touched with mine.

but in the end, all you were was my first heartbreak.

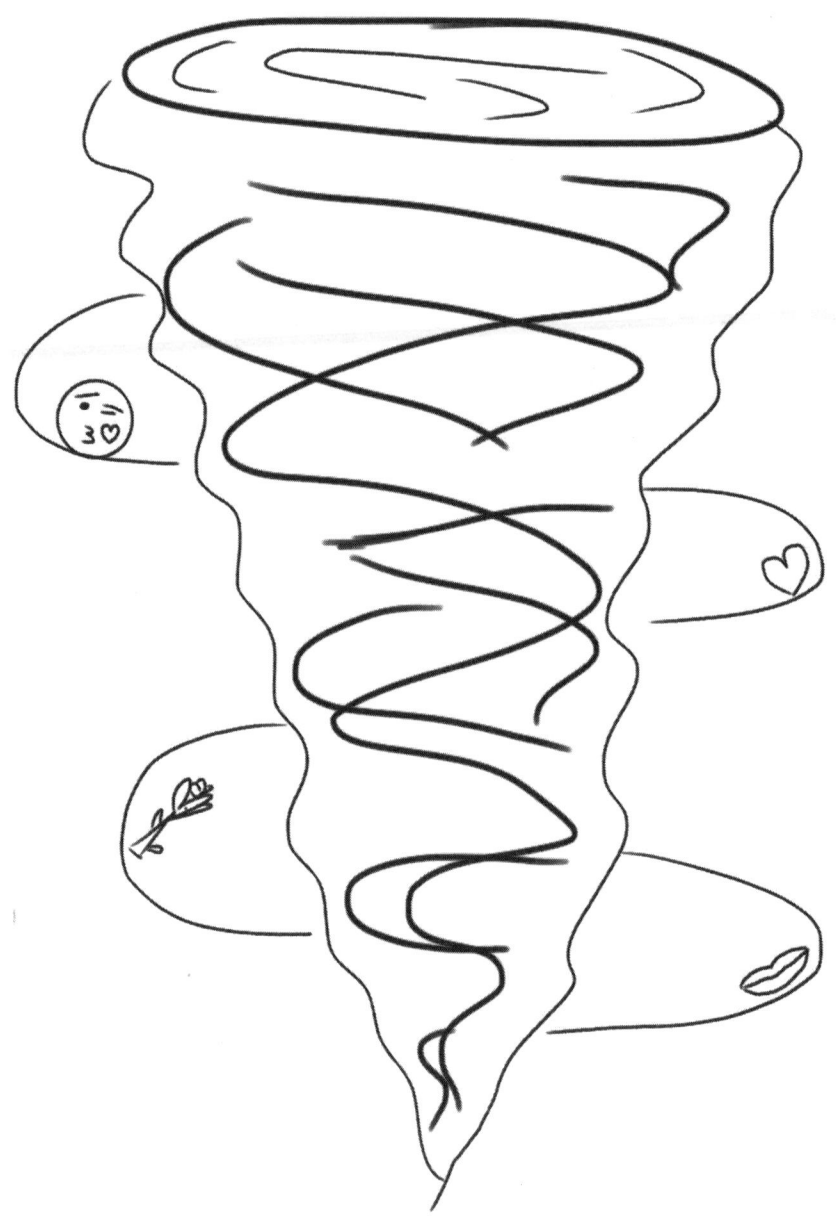

bloom.

you were my happiness.

you brought me joy.

you made me laugh.

you made me cry.

you held my hand.

you kissed me.

you made me feel special, but then you,

you dropped me.

bloom.

how can you go from loving me, to hating me that fast?

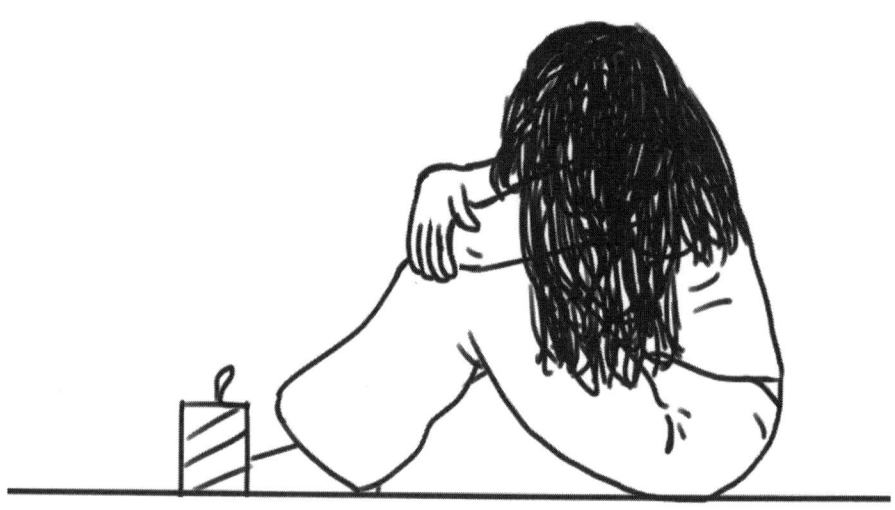

bloom.

i'm silly for thinking i was important to you.

bloom.

i was burned by you again.

i fell for that half-smile of yours.

i got caught up in our happy moments - in our giggles and jokes.

i should've known better.

i should've known you were going to break my heart.

i should've left you where i did the first time.

bloom.

you played me like a game.

it was a mind game though.

was i good enough for you?

did i make you happy?

all the challenges i had to face, to see if i was good enough for you.

but, in the end, i decided to quit the game.

and i will never play again.

bloom.

i don't quite understand what happened to us.

everything was fine, but then you met her.

she changed you and not in the right way.

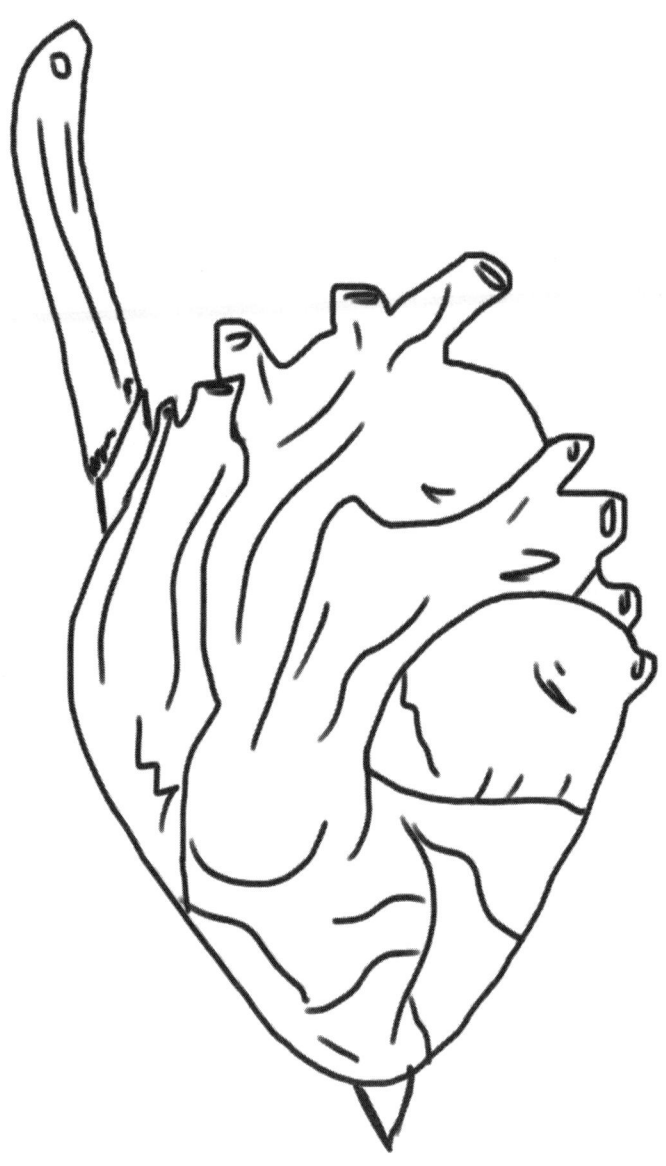

bloom.

please be gentle,

my heart is tender.

it has broken before.

shattered, some might say.

it will need care.

it will also need to be loved.

you may start to catch feelings, and that's okay, but don't love me.

you'll end up regretting it.

bloom.

i was going through our old pictures last night.

i was thinking to myself, wow, i miss this. i miss us.

but, then i remembered, all you did was cause me pain and tears,

and i don't miss that.

bloom.

i want to go back to the old us.

the old us who could laugh for hours,

we played the silliest games,

never got tired of snuggles,

always tried to impress each other,

always wanted those kisses,

always wanted to be touched,

and always wanted to be loved,

but now all i feel is us going through the motions.

bloom.

you were my favorite hello.

but, my hardest goodbye.

you were my favorite notification.

but, sometimes, you made me cry.

being in your arms was one of the greatest feelings,

but only i was dreaming.

bloom.

the loss is on you, not me.

i'm not waiting around for you anymore.

i guess if you want to talk, you will.

i end up getting hurt in the end.

you have other priorities before me.

i was a fool for telling myself i'm your priority,

but it's going to be your loss, not mine.

bloom.

the best thing, we think, is holding on to the person,

but it's actually letting the person go.

bloom.

it isn't your loss even though you think it is.

it's theirs.

they lost someone who loved and cared for them.

bloom.

i know you love me because you say so.

but, you don't show it like you used to.

you don't open doors for me.

you don't kiss me randomly.

you don't pull me close and hug me.

you don't take silly pictures with me.

you don't snuggle with me like you used to.

you don't laugh with me.

you don't check up on me.

you don't ask how i am feeling.

all you care about is your little circle.

when will you put that care in me?

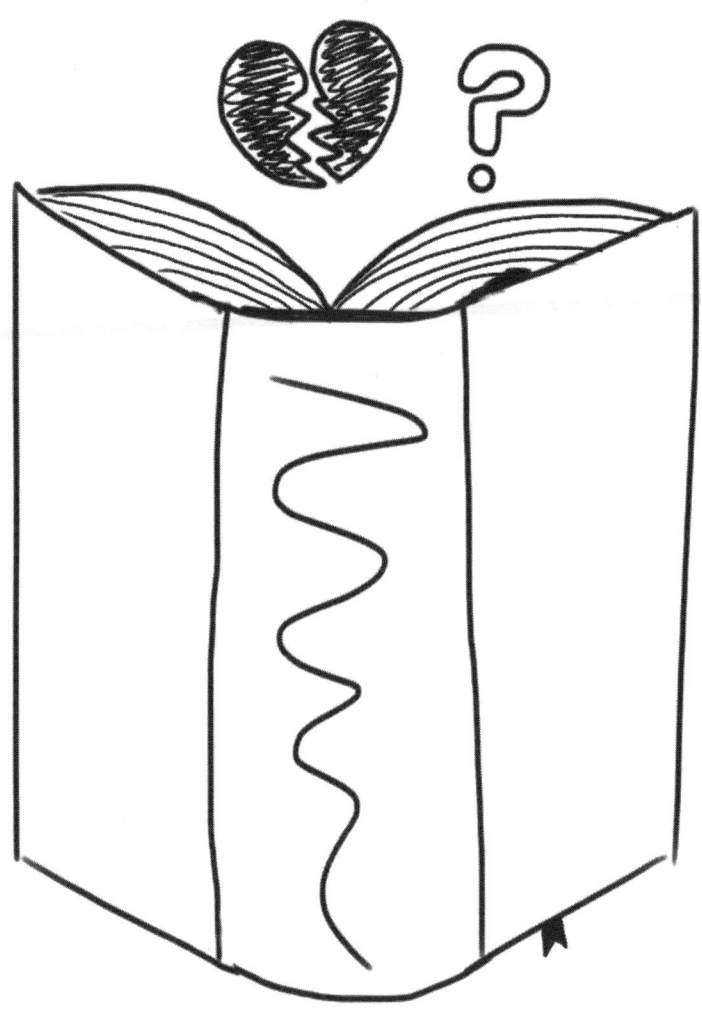

bloom.

there once was this story.

this story was kind of complicated.

it went like this, a boy and a girl fell in love.

they both knew what they felt.

but, as i am reading i wonder to myself,

how can you love someone for one minute, and then the next
you don't?

it doesn't make a whole lot of sense to me.

either you love her or leave her.

you never know what others are going through.

you know everything is going great in your life, but what
   about others?

you don't know what it's like to feel the pain they are feeling.

you don't know what it's like to have a fake smile every day.

you aren't for sure what it feels like to pretend that everything is
   going well.

you don't know what it's like listening to a person whose heart
   is breaking.

their voice is shaky, and they are trying to get the words out the
   best they can without falling apart.

you don't know how it is in a depressed and anxious mind.

but, you won't ever know until you experience it.

and then, you will understand.

bloom.

i hope when you wake up, your first thought is of me.

i hope you realize what you lost.

i hope you will see me out and about and start replaying our
    memories in your head.

i hope you go home and cry over me.

i hope you feel the pain that i have had to go through.

but, i hope you won't ever hurt her as you did me.

bloom.

take time and heal.

heal that heart of yours; it was just broken into a million pieces.

you had strong feelings.

it was love for you.

but, to him, it was nothing.

it's okay to hurt.

you loved him, but he didn't love you.

bloom.

all you ever do is hurt me, but you don't even know you do.

bloom.

i need to pull away from you.

i have a good feeling about us, but i shouldn't.

i am attached to an imaginary string that belongs to you.

whenever you need me, you can pull me in.

but, when you don't need me, you just let the string go.

it makes me hurt as a person.

it makes me feel like a horrible person and i doubt myself.

i can never be there for you whenever.

it has to be when you need something.

hope

bloom.

in the end, all of it will make sense.

bloom.

sometimes it feels like it won't get better.
but trust me, something is waiting for you.
just be patient.

bloom.

we occasionally still catch feelings.

i still catch him looking at me.

he's looking deep into me.

almost like he's looking at, something he hasn't seen before.

and well, that makes me want him even more.

bloom.

tonight, you said the words.

the words i never thought you would say to me.

it's like you planned it out.

honestly, it caught me off guard.

i can't think now.

i keep replaying the words in my head.

is it true?

do you love me?

or were they fill-in words,

the words that fit the occasion.

bloom.

don't think you owe anyone an apology for being yourself.

bloom.

you have me.

you don't have to question that.

but do i have you?

that's something i question all the time.

bloom.

she was strong.

she was a fighter.

she wanted to give up, but she knew she had a fire.

bloom.

let me be yours.

i don't want to be anyone else's.

just yours.

i'm not asking much, just some.

bloom.

girl, in the end, you are the only one who will need you.

you need to give yourself that attention, take it in, and find who

you are.

bloom.

one day you will feel happy.

one day you feel sad.

one day you feel depressed.

one day you will feel upset.

one day you're beaming with joy.

you will also feel loved.

but another day, you're super anxious.

you could become angry.

you could become adventurous.

and one day, you find enough strength to put your broken pieces

back together.

and then, you will heal.

bloom.

i wake up in the mornings thinking about you.

i'm not thinking about you in the lovey ways, i'm thinking about
   you in the "i'm praying for you" way.

i pray for you that your eyes will open someday,

and you will see all the worldly things around you.

i pray that you will see, those people that you think are "good,"
   they aren't.

i pray for you that you will meet the most amazing woman that
   you can call yours forever.

and i pray for you that one day you will turn to God,

and you will let him lead you home.

bloom.

at some point you have to let them go.

no matter how hard it is.

no matter if you want to or not.

it will seem impossible.

your heart will feel torn, and it will feel shattered.

you will most likely cry for days.

you won't be able to think straight.

all you will want is to be in their arms,

you know you can't, though, and it makes you even sadder.

but, it will eventually get better.

ten ways to cope with a broken heart...

1. cry. it's okay to cry, cry as much as you need too.

2. keep no contact with him. delete his number and unfollow him on all your social media.

3. delete the pictures of you and him. it will just make it easier to not think about him.

4. eat lots of ice cream or cookie dough. it's okay to eat it. somehow it has something that will make you feel better and comforted.

5. talk out your feelings. talk to your mom. even though you don't think she will help, she will.

6. take a nice hot bubble bath. add some extra lavender and bubbles. you will feel so relaxed.

7. cuddle your pet. somehow they know you are hurting.

8. get some fresh air. go outside and sit even. you won't want to see the daylight, but you need to have a reminder you will be okay.

9. go out with your friends. put some makeup on and your cutest outfit.

10. don't think of it as it's over, think of it as a lesson learned.

bloom.

i know you are in a much better place now.

no pain.

but, for me, it brings me pain when i hear your name.

it seems crazy because i didn't feel that close to you, but now
that i think about it, i was.

more than we both thought.

i still think about your Dairy Queen order, and i order it every
time i get ice cream.

i think about all the softball games we went to together.

i know i wasn't the only one that lost you and that others were
affected, but you left a significant impact on me.

i can't explain it.

in times, i've wanted to give up, i have kept pushing because i
know that's how you had to live.

you had to decide everyday which it was going to be, if you were
going to quit or if you were still going to put up a fight.

and i thank you for leaving behind a little of your fight for me.

bloom.

you have made it to the end of this journey. my journey. my words are now a part of you. some of these poems you might have felt and some of them not so much, and that's okay. some of these were difficult for me to write, but i decided they needed to be written so i can close some of my open doors, to share my talent, and lastly, for you to know that you are not alone with your feelings. you are heard and you are understood. may you always continue to bloom.

-from me to you

acknowledgements

first, thank you to whoever has read, seen, looked at, or touched this book, you are indeed a blessing to me.

thank you to the person(s) who have inspired these writings in my book, whether they were sad or happy writings. these writings led me to find myself and uncover a talent i didn't know i had. i have learned a lot over the last several months of this journey. going through these obstacles and this thing called life, i wouldn't trade it for anything; i am now a better person because of it all.

another thank you goes out to the people who made this all happen. thank you to Karen Schober and her team that has answered hundreds of questions and emails from me. another huge thanks to Tami Boyce for doing all the interior work on this book. you guys have been great helpers during this time. to my Mom and Dad in giving me this life, so i could discover that i have a writing talent. to others, this includes

Andy, Dawn, Jennifer, Ms. Houk, and Mrs. Reynolds for reading over my poems gazillions of times and putting your time and effort into making my work better. also, to my boyfriend that i get to call mine, Aden. you have supported me from the very beginning, when i jumped in this process with two feet, not having any idea what i was doing, but i knew you always believed in me, and i appreciate that.

a super special thanks to Aden and Andy on the amazing illustrations!

lastly, a thank you to the readers that have read this book and supported me through it all. to the ones who get me and can relate to something personal- you created that special bond between us, you didn't think you would have.

thank you again, from the bottom of my heart. this book wouldn't happen without all of you. the love and effort has taught me to take my thoughts from my notes and create something within me. i am so glad that we both have each other.

much love,
myah

about the author

Myah Davidson is a sixteen year old girl who is faithful and loves God. She lives in a small town in Illinois called Casey. She is currently a student in high school. Myah recently discovered she has a niche for writing. When Myah isn't writing, she is either cuddling her doodle Sophie and her shitz tzu Stormy, baking yummy desserts, making creative food recipes, sipping on coffee, hanging out with her gal pals, spending time with her family or boyfriend and his family, or creating new projects. This is her first book.